PRO WRESTLING LEGENDS

CHELSEA HOUSE PUBLISHERS

Mick Foley:
The Story of the Wrestler
They Call "Mankind"

Kyle Alexander

Chelsea House Publishers
Philadelphia

Produced by Chestnut Productions and Choptank Syndicate, Inc.

Editor and Picture Researcher: Mary Hull
Design and Production: Lisa Hochstein

CHELSEA HOUSE PUBLISHERS

Editor in Chief: Sally Cheney
Associate Editor in Chief: Kim Shinners
Production Manager: Pamela Loos
Art Director: Sara Davis
Director of Photography: Judy L. Hasday
Cover Illustrator: Keith Trego

Cover Photos: Howard Kernats
　　　　　　　and Jeff Eisenberg Sports Photography

The Chelsea House World Wide Web site
address is http://www.chelseahouse.com

First Printing

1 3 5 7 9 8 6 4 2

Library of Congress Cataloging-in-Publication Data

Alexander, Kyle.
　　Mick Foley: the story of the wrestler they call "Mankind" / Kyle Alexander.
　　　　p. cm. — (Pro wrestling legends)
　　Includes bibliographical references (p.) and index.
　　ISBN 0–7910–6446–8 (alk. paper) — ISBN 0–7910–6447–6 (pbk. : alk. paper)
　　　　1. Foley, Mick—Juvenile literature. 2. Wrestlers—United States—Biography—
　　Juvenile literature. [1. Foley, Mick. 2. Wrestlers.] I. Title. II. Series.

　　GV1196.F64 A44 2001
　　796.812'092—dc21
　　[B]
　　　　　　　　　　　　　　　　　　　　　　　　　　　　00–069393

Contents

1 CHAMPION OF ALL MANKIND

At the November 15, 1998, World Wrestling Federation (WWF) Survivor Series pay-per-view card, Mankind was robbed of the WWF World heavyweight title by WWF owner Vince McMahon Jr., the man he had called "Dad." Now, after more than 13 years of putting his body on the line night after night in the most dangerous matches in the world, Mankind was no longer content to wait for tomorrow. He wanted revenge.

It was December 29, 1998, in Worcester, Massachusetts. Worcester is a worn-down, blue-collar town that fit Mankind's image as a worn-down, blue-collar wrestler who would do anything in the ring for glory. On this night, though, Mankind's chances for glory looked slim. Mankind publicly begged for a WWF World title shot, but McMahon, the man who called the shots, refused.

"You've had your chances," McMahon said. "If you had listened to me all along, you'd be the number one contender right now."

Those words angered Mankind, but not nearly as much as what McMahon said next: The owner of the WWF accused him of not paying his dues. The words grated against Mankind's soul. Not paid his dues? He had lost part of his ear while

---

Mankind points to the Rock, who has something he wants: the WWF World heavyweight championship belt.

7

Fellow Vince McMahon foe Steve Austin rushed to Mankind's aid and helped him defeat the Rock for the WWF World title on December 29, 1998.

wrestling in Germany! He had nearly lost his life after getting powerbombed onto a concrete floor! He had taken death-defying leaps through tables!

He had far more than his fair share of scars to prove that he had paid his dues. Now he wanted the reward.

But even on this night, the reward wouldn't come easy. Later in the card, Mankind lost to Hunter Hearst Helmsley in a match in which Shane McMahon, Vince's son, was special guest referee. When Shane made a fast count on the pin, Mankind placed the younger McMahon in a submission hold. Vince and his cronies came running out to save Shane, but this time, Mankind held the upper hand: "If you don't give me a world title match later in the card, I'll break Shane's shoulder," Mankind said. Vince McMahon had no choice but to give in. Mankind had held the WWF hostage.

The reigning world champion was exactly the person Mankind wanted: Rocky Maivia, better known as the Rock, who had been the beneficiary of Mankind's setback at the Survivor Series. The Rock was backed by McMahon's Team Corporate, but Mankind had an equally lethal group on his side: D-Generation X.

After the opening bell, Mankind and Maivia took their brawl outside the ring. They punished each other with forearms and kicks, and, in a bizarre match twist, even took time out to provide television color commentary while they fought. Later in the match, the Rock scored with his "people's elbow" elbowsmash, then smashed the world title belt over Mankind's head. Mankind pulled a sweatsock onto his right hand and tried to apply his "mandible claw" submission hold, but Ken Shamrock ran into the ring and hit him with a chair. Mankind lay motionless on the mat.

Mankind, however, had friends on his side. "Stone Cold" Steve Austin, his former tag team partner, rushed to the rescue and slammed the Rock with a chair. Now both men were laying in the ring. Austin placed Mankind on top of Maivia. The referee made the three-count. Mankind was the WWF World heavyweight champion.

Mankind's childhood dream had come true. He had proven to the world that he wasn't merely a hardcore wrestler, he was a champion. Mankind grabbed the microphone and delivered a special message to his son and daughter.

"At the risk of not sounding very cool," he said, "I want to dedicate this match to my two little ones at home. Big Daddio did it!"

The McMahons were irate. They had learned the hard way that Mankind couldn't be stopped. Anybody who had followed his career, though, knew that all along.

TRUTH OR CONSEQUENCES

He was not born in a dungeon. He was not born in Truth or Consequences, New Mexico. He was not the psychotic child of a deranged scientist. And he certainly wasn't neglected.

Mankind, Cactus Jack, and Dude Love would have you believe a lot of fictional things about themselves—or, more correctly, himself—but the truth of the matter is simple: The wrestler known as Mankind, Cactus Jack, and Dude Love was born Mick Foley on June 7, 1965, and had a normal childhood.

His mother was the first member of her family to attend college. She went to the State University of New York at Brockport and got her masters from the State University of New York at Stony Brook on Long Island. She taught physical education in East Setauket, also on Long Island, where she met her future husband, Jack Foley.

Jack Foley was the director of physical education for the Long Island school system that included Ward Melville High School, which his son Mick Foley later attended. Mr. Foley was the chairman of high school basketball and lacrosse in Suffolk County, New York, and he was known as a tough, hardworking man. He'd get up before dawn and work until after the sun went down. He read newspapers voraciously, at

---

Calling himself "Cactus Jack," Mick Foley made his pro debut in Clarksburg, West Virginia, in 1986. The announcer told the crowd he was from Truth or Consequences, New Mexico.

least two a day during the week and four on Sundays.

After getting married, the Foleys' had their first child, John, in 1964. Mick was born a year later. Although Jack Foley worked long hours, he managed to form a close relationshp with his sons. Jack was always attending some kind of high school sporting event, either as a coach or a spectator, and he often allowed his sons to tag along. Jack also took his sons to Yankee Stadium to watch the baseball games. Mick's hero was catcher Thurman Munson.

But with his father gone so often, Mick had to find ways to entertain himself . . . and other people. Mick realized at an early age that he loved to entertain people, so when he and his friends formed a neighborhood whiffle ball league, it wasn't enough for them to just play, they had to have an audience. Mothers, fathers, brothers, sisters, and friends would show up to watch the Parsonage Pirates with the chunky five-year-old catcher named Mick. They played in a vacant lot next to a neighbor's house.

Mick was a natural athlete, and he excelled at baseball and lacrosse. Not surprisingly, considering how he turned out, Mick was fearless. He played the most dangerous positions: catcher in baseball and goaltender in lacrosse. Of course his size helped him play those positions. Mick was always an oversized teenager.

He was fearless, too. As Foley said in his autobiography, *Have a Nice Day*, he once taunted a counselor at the lacrosse camp he attended in Suffolk County. Tension built between the two boys, and they decided to settle their differences with a boxing match. They wore lacrosse helmets and gloves for protection. Mick's opponent hit him hard with a few well-placed punches, and the bout was stopped. Mick, bleeding badly, was obviously the loser.

Prior to his senior year at Ward Melville High School, Mick decided to go out for the track team to get in shape for lacrosse season.

"If you want to get in shape, there's nothing better than wrestling," his friend John McNulty advised him.

"I've never wrestled a match in my whole life," Mick replied.

"Well, you've been around wrestling your whole life, and you've wrestled your brother, who's a good wrestler."

Mick thought it over. He had always enjoyed watching pro wrestling on TV. Jimmy "Superfly" Snuka was his hero. He enjoyed watching amateur wrestling, too. His older brother was, indeed, a pretty good wrestler, and he had taught him some moves. At 215 pounds, Mick certainly had the size to battle the other heavyweights in the county.

Mick went out for the team and made it. Jim McGonigle, his coach, later called him "the best first-time wrestler I ever met." In his fourth match, he beat the wrestler who was fourth in the county. Although Mick won 13 matches and lost 7 in his only season as a high school wrestler, he beat bigger and more experienced opponents and developed a love for the sport.

Mick liked wrestling so much that he didn't want to play lacrosse anymore. He had never before considered wrestling as a career, but now he found himself studying tapes of pro wrestlers. In June 1983 Mick attended his first live pro wrestling card at New York's Madison

Square Garden. The main event was Snuka vs. Magnificent Muraco. Mick was hooked.

Mick graduated from Ward Melville High School in June of 1983 and spent the summer as a lifeguard. Sitting in the hot sun, he'd dream about becoming a pro wrestler. He had applied to several colleges with the intention of playing lacrosse, but now he had no desire to play. Instead, he enrolled in the State University of New York, at the College at Cortland in upstate New York.

It was during Mick's freshman year of college that *The Legend of Frank Foley* was born.

That year, he was on a date with a fellow student named Kathy, who he thought was the girl of his dreams. He had been admiring her from afar all semester. As they walked holding hands at the end of the date, Kathy leaned over, kissed him on the cheek, and said, "Goodnight, Frank."

Mick was in despair. The woman of his dreams didn't even know his name! When he got back to his dorm room, Mick told a friend to start snapping pictures of him. Mick assembled a photo album, then decided to turn the photo essay into a movie. Using an eight-millimeter hand-held camera, Mick and his friend recreated the disastrous date. In the final scene, Mick planned on taking out his aggression on some stuffed animals.

"Let's make this realistic," Mick declared.

He filled his mouth with red food coloring, leaped off the bed, came down onto the stuffed animal with a perfectly placed elbowsmash, and allowed the food coloring to spray across the room. The people watching this were disgusted, but that was exactly the reaction he wanted.

With *The Legend of Frank Foley*, Mick had learned the value of bleeding for a wrestling audience.

Mick got his big break in March 1985 during his sophomore year at Cortland College. His alma mater, Ward Melville High School, sponsored an independent wrestling show, and, of course, Jack Foley planned to attend. Shortly before the card, Mick got a call from his father.

"I talked to the promoter," Jack Foley said. "He said that if you come to the show, he'll talk to you about becoming a wrestler."

Mick drove five hours from Cortland to Ward Melville High. When he got to the high school,

Mick Foley's wrestling idol was Jimmy "Superfly" Snuka, one of the great aerial artists of wrestling. As a kid, Foley never dreamed that he would one day get to wrestle with Snuka.

his father introduced him to promoter Tommy Dee. Tommy told Mick that if he were willing to work with his ring crew, delivering and setting up the rings at his shows, he would have one of his veteran wrestlers teach him some moves. Mick agreed. Every few weeks, he would drive from Cortland to New York City to pick up the ring and deliver it to the arena in which it would be used. Dominic "Dee" DeNucci, the former WWF World tag team champion, taught him how to wrestle.

By mid-December, Mick had helped Dee a dozen times, but he had been in the ring only four times. He was getting better, but not fast enough for his liking. Finally, DeNucci invited Mick to train with him at his club in suburban Pittsburgh.

Mick made the 800-mile round trip from Cortland to Freedom, Pennsylvania, at least 70 times during his final year and a half in college. DeNucci's school was located in the gym of Freedom Elementary School, and the first time he was there, Mick was slammed and tossed around for hours. At first Mick hated wrestling, but he refused to quit. He didn't want to be a failure. Although he never told his friends what he was doing or where he was going, he spent every weekend in Freedom. While his friends were studying and having a good time, Mick was getting bumped, bruised, and abused by DeNucci and the other wrestlers, and he was paying $25 a day for the privilege.

Mick enjoyed the weekly training sessions. He also did well in school, where he was study-ing radio and television production. He won the Anne Allen Award as the outstanding student in his major.

After his junior year at Cortland, Mick moved to Pittsburgh for the summer to train. On June 24, 1986, Mick appeared on his first professional wrestling card at the Clarksburg Armory in Clarksburg, West Virginia. He was supposed to wrestle in a battle royal, but plans changed at the last minute, and Mick was thrown into a singles match against Kurt Kaufman. As Foley tells it in *Have a Nice Day*, before the match, ring announcer Hank Hudson asked him, "What's your name?"

"Cactus Jack," Mick said.

"Where are you from, Cactus Jack?" Hudson said.

"Bloomington, Indiana."

"I don't think there are any cactuses in Indiana. What about Arizona?"

"Okay," Mick said. "Is Tucson, Arizona, good?"

But Hudson, a postal worker, knew about a lot of places, and suggested a different hometown: Truth or Consequences, New Mexico. Mick thought that sounded great: Cactus Jack from Truth or Consequences, New Mexico.

Cactus Jack made his ring debut that night and lost.

It was something he'd have to get used to.

3   CACTUS JACK

I n 1986 pro wrestling was hot, and the WWF was the hottest promotion in pro wrestling. But when Dominic DeNucci told Mick in mid-August that Vince McMahon needed some extra wrestlers for a television taping in Providence, Rhode Island, and Hartford, Connecticut, Mick didn't exactly jump for joy.

From his earliest days in the sport, Mick Foley understood pro wrestling. He understood that a wrestler's image was his most important asset. Sure, appearing on a televised WWF card would be great publicity and exposure, but he didn't want to be exposed as a loser, and he was certain that losing to a far more talented and experienced opponent would be the extent of his appearances on WWF television.

Still, it's not easy to say no to an opportunity like this, and at the time, it was nearly impossible for an aspiring wrestler to say no to Vince McMahon. Foley, along with several of DeNucci's wrestlers (including Troy Martin, who would come to be known as Extreme Championship Wrestling (ECW) world heavyweight champion Shane Douglas), traveled to New England for their first chance in the big-time spotlight.

Mick felt intimidated by all of the stars at the Providence Civic Center that first night. These were people he had

---

In promotions like the UWF, the CWA, the CWF, and WCW, Cactus Jack developed a reputation as a physically tough wrestler who could endure grueling matches.

watched on TV, and now he was going to wrestle one of them—two of them, as it turned out. He was teamed with Les Thornton against world tag team champions the British Bulldogs. Davey Boy and Dynamite Kid had formed one of the best tag teams in wrestling, and Mick found out why. Wrestling as Cactus Jack, he was manhandled by both men and rocked when Dynamite Kid clotheslined him across the jaw. He had never felt such intense pain. One suplex later, Cactus Jack had been pinned in his first WWF match.

Things didn't go any better the following night. With his jaw still aching, Cactus teamed with Terry Gibbs and lost a one-sided match to the Killer Bees.

Mick Foley was still in college when he competed in his first WWF match, a tag team bout that he and Les Thornton lost to the famed British Bulldogs. Because he didn't want to become known as a loser, Cactus Jack stopped wrestling for the WWF and moved to smaller federations where he could gain experience.

Although he was beaten and battered, Mick was proud that he had accomplished his dream. When he got back to Cortland, his friends, who had finally found out what Mick had been doing on weekends, gave him a hero's welcome.

During his senior year of college, Mick spent 28 out of 32 weekends training and wrestling in Freedom, Pennsylvania, and other small towns in Pennsylvania, West Virginia, and Ohio. He appeared at a few more WWF television tapings, but stopped because he didn't want to become known as a loser. He simply wasn't ready for the major leagues.

One of the highlights of his year was a show in Hundred, West Virginia, for the Universal Wrestling Federation (UWF). Mick had a great match against Troy Orndorff, and afterward was complimented by several of the UWF's veteran stars.

"You might have a future in this business," Buddy Roberts told him.

Even the surlier veterans couldn't deny that Mick had a great attitude for wrestling. He was a hardworking athlete who was willing to do anything to get a rise out of the crowd. He was fearless and always willing to put his body on the line. Mick always looked the worse for wear after his matches, but so did his opponents.

After Mick graduated from college in 1987, DeNucci gave him a spot on a wrestling tour of West Africa. Mick was supposed to get paid $1,500 a week but never saw a penny because the government of Burkina Faso was overthrown and the country was in turmoil. In six weeks, Mick went on three different tours in Africa, lost pints of blood, and made only $480. Back in the United States, he'd drive hundreds and hundreds of miles and get paid very little money to wrestle for various independent federations.

But by 1988 Mick was wrestling frequently and improving rapidly. He gained recognition on Long Island for one of his performances on promoter Mark Tendler's wrestling cards. Mick was billed as Cactus Jack from the Fiji Islands, and he teamed with King Kaluha as the South Seas Islanders. During the week Mick worked as a landscaper, bartender, and bouncer. He was making about $400 weekly, which was a fortune to him. He also taught at Tendler's wrestling school.

Mick got his next big break early in the summer of 1988, when the influential *Wrestling Observer* newsletter called him "the best no-name independent in the country." Almost immediately, he got a call from Tommy Gilbert, the father of wrestler Eddie Gilbert. Tommy was starting a small federation in Kansas City, and he wanted Mick to come out and wrestle full-time. Mick wasted no time accepting the offer. Two weeks later, when he hadn't heard back from Gilbert about a starting date, he went to Memphis, Tennessee, to wrestle in the Championship Wrestling Association (CWA).

Upon his arrival at the Mid-South Coliseum in Memphis, Cactus Jack was introduced as the newest member of Robert Fuller's Stud Stable. The Stud Stable was a rulebreaking group that, in addition to Fuller and Cactus Jack, included Jimmy Golden and "Gorgeous" Gary Young. In October 1988, Cactus Jack and Young won the CWA tag team title in Evansville, Indiana. But Mick wasn't happy in Memphis. Fuller and Golden eventually turned against

Jack and Young, who left the Stud Stable. Mick left Memphis after losing a loser-leaves-town match against the Stud Stable and getting bloodied by Fuller's kendo stick.

Next stop: Texas and the World Class promotion, which just a few years earlier, due to the ongoing war between the Fabulous Freebirds and the Von Erichs, had been a major hot spot of wrestling in the United States. Not anymore. Still, the pay was better than it had been in Memphis, and Jack and Gary Young became the top rulebreaking team in the World Class area. Their manager was General Skandor Akbar, whose stable of wrestlers was known as Devastation Incorporated. Because most of the other wrestlers in the federation—Kerry Von Erich, Eric Embry, Jeff Jarrett, Brickhouse Brown, and Chris Adams—were fan favorites, Cactus Jack had the opportunity to reveal his wild side. But Cactus Jack wasn't simply a demented psycho who tore apart everything in his path. To the fans, he was naïve and simple-minded.

Cactus Jack took his share of lumps in Texas. One night, he teamed with Akbar in a scaffold match against Embry and Percy Pringle in Fort Worth. In a scaffold match the wrestlers battle on a narrow platform high above the ring. The object is to push your opponent off the scaffold. It's one of the most dangerous matches in the world. When Embry kicked him off the scaffold, Cactus Jack careened face-first toward the mat far below. He put his hand down to block the fall, and landed in a heap. Cactus screamed out in pain. He suffered a broken bone in his left wrist. He remained in a cast for 16 weeks, but kept wrestling the entire time. In fact, it was during this period that Cactus Jack developed his signature maneuver: a flying elbowsmash off the ring apron and onto his prone opponent lying on the arena floor.

But with the injury came losses and mounting concern about his career. Looking to the future—and what it might hold for him—Mick started learning about editing and working on television wrestling programs. He briefly got his hopes up when he heard that Jim Ross was interested in bringing him to World Championship Wrestling (WCW), but his hopes were dashed when Ross resigned two weeks later. After nine months in Texas, he lost his final match to Eric Embry in nine seconds and hit the road. So began a tumultuous period in Mick Foley's career.

His first stop after leaving Texas in 1989 was Montgomery, Alabama, and the Continental Wrestling Federation (CWF), but the CWF was in deep financial trouble and about to shut down. At about this time, Mick got a call from Shane Douglas, who was wrestling in WCW. Douglas convinced Mick to attend a WCW TV taping at the Center Stage Theater in Atlanta. He met WCW executives and was invited to come back and wrestle two weeks later. In his first TV match, Cactus Jack was destroyed by Rick and Scott Steiner. It was like the WWF experience all over again.

But the loss to the Steiners impressed some important people. Every time the Steiners clotheslined him, Cactus got back up and invited more punishment. After Cactus and his partner lost the match, Cactus attacked his partner, pummeled him with forearm smashes,

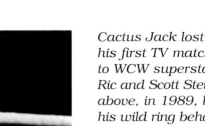

Cactus Jack lost his first TV match to WCW superstars Ric and Scott Steiner, above, in 1989, but his wild ring behavior and his refusal to give up easily got him noticed.

and sent him flying to the arena floor. Then Cactus climbed onto the ring apron and delivered a sensational flying elbowsmash onto his partner's prone body.

"You were the star of the match," announcer Joe Pedicino told him.

Cactus Jack was invited back for the next TV tapings in Greensboro and Raleigh, North Carolina in 1989. After losing a match to Tommy Rich and Ranger Ross, Cactus clotheslined partner Ned Brady over the top rope, then delivered his flying elbowsmash off the apron. The next night in Raleigh, Cactus lost a great match against Flyin' Brian Pillman. After the match, Cactus was attacked by Sting.

Kevin Sullivan became Cactus's manager in 1989, and they were a demented pair. Sullivan loved inflicting pain on his opponents. Cactus would stand at ringside during matches reading the book *I Am in Urgent Need of Advice.* Cactus feuded with Mike Rotundo, Norman the Lunatic, and Abdullah the Butcher. He also teamed with Rotundo.

The next turning point in Mick's career occurred at Clash of the Champions X on February 6, 1990, in Corpus Christi, Texas. His opponent was masked Mexican wrestling legend Mil Mascaras. Late in the match Cactus threw Mascaras outside the ring, then picked him up into a backbreaker. Cactus dropped Mascaras to the floor and prepared for a flying elbowsmash, but Mascaras snuck back into the ring, dropkicked Cactus, and sent him crashing hard to the arena floor. On television, announcers Jim Ross and Jim Cornette were predicting that Cactus's career was over. There seemed to be no way he could get up after absorbing such an impact on a concrete floor.

But Cactus Jack did get up, and although he was eventually pinned, he had sent a message to the wrestling world: "I can take as much punishment as you can dish out."

Cactus Jack had become a cult favorite. Fans loved watching him wrestle. He had an intense feud with Norman the Lunatic, in which both men spilled plenty of blood and suffered plenty of bruises. He also formed an impressive tag team with 400-pound madman Abdullah the Butcher. Cactus and Abdullah had at least one thing in common: Neither of them played by the conventional rules.

Cactus, however, felt passed over in WCW. He didn't think he was getting the attention he deserved. He suspected that if he didn't make a move soon, within a year he'd be wrestling at the bottom rung of WCW, and possibly be out of a job entirely. Cactus had to face facts: The WCW promoters considered him to be nothing more than a punching bag.

So he gambled. In 1990 he left WCW (and his $1,000 a week salary) and returned to the independent circuit, where he was certain to make far less money than he had been making. Mick Foley was gambling on Cactus Jack's future.

TWISTED FATE

Do you believe in fate? Well, consider this: If Mick Foley hadn't taken a gamble and left WCW, he would have never been at Riverhead Raceway on Long Island in the fall of 1990. He would have been miles away, wrestling in the southern states for WCW. If he wasn't at Riverhead Raceway, he would never have met his future wife, a beautiful woman and former model named Collette Christie.

"Could you speak to her on my behalf," Mick asked a friend. "I'd like to meet her."

They met. They went out on a date. They fell in love. Soon, they got married. In 1992, their first son, Francis Dewey Foley, was born in Massapequa, Long Island, New York.

Fate.

And if Mick Foley hadn't left WCW, he never would have had the chance to wrestle his boyhood idol, Jimmy "Superfly" Snuka, on a Universal Wrestling Federation (UWF) card. They battled to a double-countout.

In March 1991 Mick gained international acclaim for the first time when he spent a month in Japan, wrestling for various promotions as Cactus Jack. The fans loved his daredevil style. Cactus frequently dove into the crowd. Legendary wrestler Stan Hansen, a tough guy and a frequent competitor

---

Throughout his career, from his reckless wrestling style to his frequent switching of federations, Mick Foley has never been afraid to take chances and look for new opportunities.

in Japan, took him under his wing and taught him the ins and outs of wrestling in Japan.

Back in the United States, Cactus had some bloody, spectacular matches with Eddie Gilbert in Philadelphia's Tri-State Wrestling Association. A barbed-wire match between Gilbert and Cactus was ruled a no-contest when a bloody Cactus got trapped in the barbed wire. Gilbert lost his share of blood, too.

The Gilbert-Cactus feud was the hottest in Tri-State. They met again in a best-of-three-falls match on August 3, 1991, at Tri-State's "Summer Sizzler" card at Pennsylvania Hall in Philadelphia. The first bout was a falls-count-anywhere match. Gilbert pinned Cactus after a clothesline from the top turnbuckle. The second match was a stretcher match. Cactus and Gilbert tried to cripple each other. Cactus threw a trash can into the ring, from which Gilbert removed a glass soda bottle, which he smashed over Cactus's head. Cactus was carried back to the dressing room on a stretcher, but the referee had already called for a double-disqualification. The final match was fought inside a steel cage. Gilbert drew blood from Cactus at the start. Both men tried to cripple each other. With Cactus in trouble, Doug Gilbert, Eddie's brother, stormed the ring, climbed the cage, and helped Eddie batter Cactus into submission. The referee ruled the match a double-disqualification.

News of the Cactus Jack vs. Eddie Gilbert war spread quickly. Both men were invited back to WCW. Gilbert declined. Cactus accepted.

More confident than ever, Cactus Jack returned to WCW after 14 months on the independent circuit. At Clash of the Champions XVI

Vader, shown wrestling with Mankind in the WWF, also wrestled Cactus Jack in a series of dangerous WCW matches that left Cactus severely injured.

on September 5, 1991, in Augusta, Georgia, U.S. champion Sting was battling Johnny B. Badd when, midway through the match, a gift-wrapped refrigerator box with a big red bow on top was wheeled down the ramp to the ring. Cactus burst from the box and attacked Sting, leaving him prone on the arena floor. Cactus mounted the ring apron and dropped his flying elbow into Sting's midsection.

Later in the night Cactus was being interviewed when another gift-wrapped box was rolled out. Sting burst from the box and hiptossed Cactus, sending him flying over the five-foot-high ramp and crashing to the arena floor. Amazingly, Cactus got up, hit Sting with a metal garbage can, and then emptied its contents over Sting's head.

WCW awarded Cactus a contract beyond his wild imagination: $156,000 a year, the most he had ever made. He continued his feud with Sting, but failed to win the U.S. title in a series of brutal cage matches.

Cactus's reckless style started taking a toll on his body. In December 1991, for example, he suffered a concussion during a tag team match. Despite his frequent visits to the doctor's—and X-ray technicians—Cactus refused to take a step backward. At Clash of the Champions XVIII on January 21, 1992, in Topeka, Kansas, Cactus stepped into the ring for a falls-count-anywhere match against Van Hammer. Shortly after the opening bell, Cactus tossed Hammer out of the ring, rolled back the protective padded mat covering the arena floor, and flipped himself through the air, into Hammer, and onto the concrete floor—from the top turn-buckle. Nobody could tell who was hurt worse, Hammer or Cactus. The two men brawled down the runway and outside the arena. Cactus hit Hammer with a police barricade and a traffic pylon. The match spilled into rodeo cattle stalls. Cactus tried to pin Hammer on a bale of hay. Hammer slammed Cactus against the metal stalls.

Suddenly, a 400-pound black cowboy carrying a shovel stormed into the rodeo area. Cactus ducked out of the way as the cowboy struck Hammer with the shovel. The "cowboy" turned out to be Abdullah the Butcher. After Cactus pinned Hammer next to a pile of horse manure, he and Abdullah continued brawling near the stalls.

Cactus and Abdullah fought in falls-count-anywhere matches throughout the WCW circuit. On February 2, 1992, Abdullah beat Cactus in a bloody steel cage match. This extremely violent series of matches compelled *Pro Wrestling Illustrated Weekly* to write, "What these two bloodthirsty goons are doing to each other is not sport. If they want to rip each other to shreds, let them do it in some back alley."

At SuperBrawl II on February 29, 1992, after Ron Simmons pinned Cactus, Abdullah stormed the ring and helped Cactus batter Simmons. Junkyard Dog raced out of the audience to save Simmons. Cactus and Abdullah were back together.

At Wrestle War '92 on May 7 in Jacksonville, Florida, Cactus and Mr. Hughes were scheduled to wrestle against Junkyard Dog and Ron Simmons. Cactus attacked Junkyard Dog on the runway leading to the ring, slammed him on the floor, and delivered a flying elbow that sent Junkyard Dog to the medical room for attention. People were starting to ask—and rightfully so—"Does Cactus Jack care about wrestling, or does he only care about hurting people?"

People asked that same question again after Sting beat Cactus in a violent match at Beach Blast '92. After the match, Cactus attacked Rick Steamboat, who was being interviewed. That started another feud. At Clash of the Champions XX in Atlanta, Cactus nearly broke his pelvis when he delivered and partially missed a flying elbowsmash onto Ron Simmons, who was laying on the concrete floor.

One thing, however, couldn't be disputed: Cactus was all about action. When Cactus attacked the hated Big Van Vader during a match against Paul Orndorff, he was suddenly all about being a fan favorite again.

Cactus and Orndorff met again in a falls-count-anywhere match on February 21, 1993, in Asheville, North Carolina. The match hadn't even started when Cactus attacked Orndorff with a shovel. Orndorff hauled Cactus to the back of the arena, tossed him over the ring barrier, then pounded on Cactus's injured knee. Orndorff threw Cactus back into the ring, removed his knee brace, and pounded on the knee joint. Then he attacked Cactus with a chair. As Cactus rolled around the canvas in pain, Orndorff threw down the chair and motioned that he was going to piledrive Cactus on top of it. Cactus reached outside the ring, grabbed his shovel, and hit Orndorff on the top of the head to get the pin.

Cactus was finally getting the recognition he had long desired. After years of toiling in anonymity, he was becoming a star. And when Big Van Vader won the world title on March 17, 1993, Cactus set his sights on winning the world title.

It nearly cost him his life.

They met for the first time on April 6 at the Center Stage Theater in Atlanta. Vader dished out a horrific beating, raining forearm smashes across Cactus's face and breaking his nose. Cactus's face was crimson with blood, but he somehow managed to win by countout. He suffered a broken nose and needed 27 stitches to close his facial wounds.

Vader was ruthless. He had already seriously injured four other wrestlers: Sting, Joe Thurman, Nikita Koloff, and Simmons. Now he wanted to destroy Cactus Jack.

They met again at the Center Stage Theater on April 21, 1993. Cactus and Vader battled outside the ring. At one point in the brutally fought contest, Cactus hurled his body at Vader and landed outside the ring, on the protective blue mats covering the concrete floor. Then

Vader's manager, Harley Race, peeled back the mat, revealing the concrete beneath. The crowd looked on in horror as Vader lifted the helpless Cactus to shoulder height and power-bombed him onto the concrete floor. The sickening thud of skin and bones striking cement filled the building. Cactus lost all feeling in his right foot and hand. WCW officials ordered the crowd to remain seated until the ambulance came. Cactus lay on his back, waiting for 40 minutes. When the ambulance arrived, Cactus was fitted with a neck brace and placed on a stretcher. He was taken to nearby hospital, where doctors diagnosed him as having suffered a severe concussion.

"He's a very lucky man," said Mike Weber, director of information services for WCW. "I'm

In 1999 former NWA champion Harley Race, who cultivated many wrestlers, including Lex Luger and Vader, founded the Harley Race Wrestling Academy and World League Wrestling, a family based promotion that focused on wrestling, not the risqué story-lines, profanity, and nudity that had come to dominate WCW and the WWF.

told that if the point of impact had been off an inch either way, Cactus could've suffered paralysis or permanent brain damage. He'll feel the effects of this for a long time, but at least he'll have all of his senses. In this case, pain is a good sign."

Cactus issued a statement through WCW officials: "I don't quite remember what happened, but I know how I feel and I know it was Vader. It might be my problem now, but it's going to be his problem before long. Vader's dealing with a man who doesn't care about pain. If it wasn't for these doctors, I'd have been out of here days ago. Vader and Race can go into hiding if they want to, but it won't help them. I'll find them wherever they flee to, and I'll gain my revenge."

Cactus's opportunity for revenge arrived at Halloween Havoc on October 24, 1993, at the Lakefront Arena in New Orleans. The bout was a Texas Death match, which doesn't end until one man decides he can't continue.

"This will be my night," Cactus told *Pro Wrestling Illustrated Weekly*. "There'll be no rules, and Vader will pay the price. He's gonna feel lots of pain at Halloween Havoc when I get my revenge."

The match started outside the ring. Cactus smashed Vader with a chair and a fan's camera. Bloody, Cactus suplexed Vader onto the runway, then they battled to a mock graveyard setup near the dressing room. Both men fell into a grave marked "R.I.P. Vader." Cactus got out, followed by a bloody Vader. Cactus clotheslined Vader and got the first fall. After a brief rest, Cactus knocked Vader from the runway to the arena floor, then scored with a flying elbowsmash for another pin. Vader took the match into the crowd and smashed Cactus repeatedly onto a chair. Then he used a moonsault, a backward somersault from the turnbuckle, to pin Cactus. Both men used chairs on each other in the next fall. Vader scored another pin. Cactus stunned Vader on the runway with a DDT, a move in which one man wraps his arm around his opponent's neck then, using a fast sit-down motion, drives the opponent's head into the floor. When Cactus got back to his feet, Race stunned his leg with an electric prodder. Vader got up before the 10-count and was declared the winner. Cactus had failed to exact revenge.

Amidst all the ongoing carnage, there was a bit of good news for Cactus Jack. On December 15, 1993, his second child, a daughter named Noelle Margaret, was born. A few months later, in March 1994 he lost part of his ear during a match against Vader in Germany. In May 1994 he and Kevin Sullivan had a spectacular feud against the Nasty Boys and beat them for the WCW World tag team title, but they lost the belts two months later on July 17. Quickly, his relationship with Sullivan went sour. Once again dissatisfied with the direction his career had taken, Cactus gave WCW officials four months' notice that he was leaving WCW. At Fall Brawl '94 on September 18, Cactus lost a loser-leaves-WCW bout to Sullivan. He walked out of WCW that night, never to return.

5 THE TOP OF THE WORLD

I f ever there was a wrestler and a wrestling federation made for each other, Cactus Jack and Extreme Championship Wrestling (ECW) were the pair. The Philadelphia-based ECW is the self-proclaimed House of Hardcore, the home of extreme, no rules, falls-count-anywhere wrestling.

Cactus Jack's introduction to ECW took place at ECW Arena in Philadelphia on June 24, 1994, before he left WCW. His opponent was Sabu, another extreme wrestler who would do anything to please the fans.

When the match started, Sabu dragged Cactus to a table outside the ring barrier. Sabu then mounted the ropes and executed a moonsault that carried him over the ring barrier and onto the table. Cactus rolled out of the way. Sabu crashed to the concrete floor. Cactus used a frying pan taken from a fan in the front row and attacked Sabu, then threw a trash can at Sabu, who pulled a glass bottle out of the garbage and broke it over Cactus's head. Paul E. Dangerously, Sabu's manager, smashed Cactus over the head with his cellular phone. Sabu got the pin, but they battled for another 10 minutes throughout the arena.

Cactus officially signed with ECW late in the summer of 1994 and made an immediate impact. On August 27 he and

In the persona of Mankind, Mick Foley struggles with Billy Gunn as they compete for the WWF World tag team title.

Mikey Whipwreck teamed to beat Public Enemy for the ECW tag team title. They lost the belts to Public Enemy on November 5, 1994.

Cactus Jack and Sabu renewed their rivalry, and Cactus beat Sabu in a falls-count-anywhere match. ECW fans loved Cactus Jack because of his reckless style. He was one of the most unorthodox fan favorites the sport had ever seen.

In the mid-1990s ECW ran only four shows a month, so Cactus had plenty of time to wrestle in other places. He won the Ozark Mountain Wrestling title. He worked for Smoky Mountain Wrestling in Tennessee. And he spent 10 days a month in Japan, where he frequently wrestled against Terry Funk, and became known as the King of the Death Match.

The term "death match" nearly took on a literal meaning on October 28, 1995, when Cactus battled Tommy Dreamer at ECW Arena. After the match, in which Dreamer pinned Cactus, Cactus tossed a burning chair, which had a gasoline-soaked towel wrapped around it, toward the ropes. The towel flew off the chair and landed on the back of Terry Funk, who had seconded Dreamer for the match. Funk's shirt and pants caught on fire. He grabbed the towel and tossed it into the first row of fans. Then the arena lights went out and stayed out for two minutes. Several fans ran for the exits. People were terrified. One fan tried to put out the fire with his hands. Then several men ran over with fire extinguishers and started spraying the fire. A few fans were hit by the extinguisher fumes. Several other fans rushed to the exit.

Funk was taken to the hospital and treated for second- and third-degree burns on his left arm and shoulders. Fortunately, no fans were injured. The match brought bad publicity to Cactus and ECW.

Cactus and Mikey Whipwreck had one more run as ECW tag team champions. On December 29, 1995, in Rego Park, New York, Whipwreck beat 2 Cold Scorpio, who had been TV champion and coholder of the tag belts with the Sandman. The match stipulation was that if Whipwreck won, he'd become TV champion and tag team champion. Whipwreck named Cactus as his cochampion. They lost the belts to the Eliminators on February 3, 1996, in Philadelphia.

Cactus Jack was as hot as he had ever been. Not surprisingly, in March 1996, the big time came calling again. This time, it was Vince McMahon Jr. and the WWF.

When Mick Foley debuted in the WWF he had a new name: Mankind. He also had a new look. A brown leather mask covered his cheeks, chin, and forehead, but kept the rest of his face exposed.

He had a new move, too: the "mandible claw," in which he jammed two of his taped-together fingers into his opponent's esophagus.

Mankind battled Undertaker and his manager, Paul Bearer, in a violent series of matches. At the June 23 King of the Ring, Mankind beat Undertaker after Bearer accidentally struck his man with the urn. Many people accused Bearer of striking Undertaker on purpose and making it look accidental. After Mankind tore through the bottom of the ring and attacked Undertaker in his match against Goldust at In Your House on July 21, Mankind and Undertaker signed for a "boiler-room brawl" at SummerSlam '96.

Meanwhile, rumors were going around the WWF that Bearer and Mankind had been seen secretly meeting. Were they in cahoots? The answer came at SummerSlam on August 18, but not before Undertaker and Mankind's violent battle.

The match started in the boiler room of Gund Arena in Cleveland, Ohio. The winner would be the first man to make it from the boiler room to the ring and claim the Undertaker's

After winning the WWF World tag team title with Mankind, Kane turned on him.

urn from Bearer, who was standing in the ring. The two men brawled in the boiler room, and Undertaker made it to the ring first. He was about to take the urn, but Bearer turned his back on him. Undertaker and Mankind continued their brawl, and when Undertaker again tried to grab the urn, Bearer hit him with it. Then he gave the urn to Mankind. Now Bearer was Mankind's manager.

"I made the Undertaker what he was, but he lost his power, and now I will do for Mankind what I did for him," Bearer said. "I will harness his powers."

But Bearer couldn't do enough harnessing. On September 22, Mankind lost to WWF World champion Shawn Michaels by disqualification in a sensational match. A few weeks later, Undertaker beat Mankind in a no-holds-barred match.

As his feud with Undertaker slowed down, Mankind turned his attention to other matters. At In Your House XII on December 15, Michaels pinned Mankind. Mankind was one of the last five men remaining in the 1997 Royal Rumble, along with the Undertaker, Bret Hart, Vader, and Steve Austin, but he was eliminated by the Undertaker after 48 minutes of action. And at WrestleMania XIII on March 23, 1997, two old rivals teamed when Mankind and Vader lost to Owen Hart and Davey Boy Smith.

After the Undertaker won the world title at WrestleMania XIII, Mankind was one of the first to take a shot at the new champion. At In Your House XIV on April 20, 1997, in Rochester, New York, the Undertaker smashed Mankind with chairs and threw him head-first into a steel guard rail and a table. Mankind grabbed a chair and beat the Undertaker. The Undertaker chokeslammed Mankind, who amazingly kicked out. But the Undertaker executed his tombstone piledriver and scored the pin.

Enter Dude Love.

Dude Love was a character from Mick Foley's childhood, from the time when he made home movies with his college friends. Starting in late May 1997, Foley did a series of interviews as Dude Love, talking about his childhood and his dreams of becoming a wrestler and about being an outcast. He described how he had always dreamed of being like Shawn Michaels. He talked about wanting people to cheer for him. He talked about being stuck in the Cactus Jack character for 11 years.

Suddenly, Mankind/Dude Love was getting cheered. A feud with Triple H improved his standing with the fans. Then, when Michaels walked out of the WWF, leaving Steve Austin without a partner, Mankind campaigned to be Austin's mate. He wore a sign that said, "Pick Me Steve," and took more punishment than ever to prove to Austin how tough he was. On July 14, 1997, at *Monday Night Raw* in San Antonio, Texas, Austin introduced Dude Love as his mystery partner. In their first match, Austin and Love teamed to beat Owen Hart and Davey Boy Smith for the world tag team title.

For the next several months, he wrestled as Mankind and Dude Love. Sometimes he appeared on the same show and wrestled in separate matches as both men. In a steel cage match against Helmsley at SummerSlam '97, Mankind was taking a beating from Triple-H when Chyna threw a steel chair into the cage.

Dude Love, one of Mick Foley's many personas, occasionally appeared in place of Mankind and even teamed with Steve Austin to capture the WWF World tag team title.

Triple-H tried to ram Mankind into the chair, but Mankind countered and sent Triple-H careening into the cage where Chyna was standing. As Mankind tried to leave the cage, Chyna slammed the door in his face. Triple-H came at him, but Mankind ducked and DDT'd him on a steel chair. Mankind climbed the cage to the top, ripped off his Mankind mask, threw it into the ring, and tore off his shirt to reveal Dude Love's red heart tattoo. With the crowd cheering, Dude Love dove into the ring on top of Triple-H. Then he climbed over the cage before Chyna dragged Triple-H out of the cage door.

Mick Foley was full of surprises. On September 22 at Madison Square Garden,

Triple-H expected to wrestle Dude Love in a falls-count-anywhere match, but neither Dude Love nor Mankind showed up. Instead, Cactus Jack made his first appearance in the WWF. They battled outside the ring for most of the match. Cactus sprayed Triple-H with a fire extinguisher, then piledrived him through a table and got the pin.

A wrestler with three alter egos had never been seen in wrestling and took the sport by storm. But, as had been the case in WCW, Cactus Jack started getting a reputation as man who fought exciting matches and took a lot of punishment, but wasn't world championship material. Cactus Jack teamed with Terry Funk to form a hardcore tag team and feuded with the New Age Outlaws, but their world title hopes came up short. Then came a turning point in wrestling history.

For two years WCW's *Nitro* had been beating the WWF's *Raw* in the Monday night cable television ratings. That changed in April 1998, thanks to an offbeat feud between new world champion Steve Austin and WWF owner Vince McMahon.

At the April 13, 1998, *Raw*, McMahon was supposed to wrestle Austin, but Dude Love prevented the match from happening. He grabbed the microphone and said, "We are tight, Steve-O, about as tight as two cats can be. But you got to understand, Steve-O, Vince McMahon writes the checks that let the Dude live the kind of life that the Dude likes to live. So I guess you could say, 'Uncle Vinny, you are my main man.'"

Dude Love became McMahon's not-so-secret weapon in his war against Austin. Love battled Austin at Unforgiven on April 26, 1998 in Greensboro, North Carolina. A few minutes into the match, McMahon's corporate associates, Pat Patterson and Jerry Brisco, walked to ringside. When Love caught Austin in an abdominal stretch, McMahon was about to call for the bell when Austin reversed the hold. When the referee got knocked out, Dude applied the mandible claw. McMahon tried to revive the referee, but couldn't. Austin knocked down Dude, smashed McMahon with a chair, covered Dude for the pin, and made the count himself. Dude won, however, when Austin was disqualified for hitting McMahon.

Austin and Dude Love battled again at Over The Edge on May 31 in Milwaukee. McMahon was the guest referee, Pat Patterson was the guest ring announcer, and Jerry Brisco was the timekeeper. The deck was stacked high against Austin, but Stone Cold won the match after the Undertaker chokeslammed Patterson, who had tried to interfere.

Austin vs. McMahon and Dude Love became the hottest feud in wrestling. *Raw* shot to the top of the cable ratings.

Mankind also returned and renewed his feud with the Undertaker. Their "Hell in the Cell" match on June 28, 1998, at the King of the Ring in Pittsburgh, was one of the most brutal matches ever fought. The Undertaker finally scored the pin, but Mankind had put on a memorable display of courage.

Either as Mankind or Dude Love, Mick Foley's star was rising fast. On July 13, 1998, Mankind teamed with Kane to beat Billy Gunn and Jesse James for the world tag team title. They would lose and regain the belts one more time before the tag team fell apart: Kane, as it turned out, was in cahoots with the Undertaker, his alleged brother.

The McMahon vs. Austin war continued. Mankind got a spot in several four-way matches against Austin that also included Kane and the Undertaker. McMahon was doing everything in his power to strip Austin of the belt, and Mankind/Dude Love was doing everything to help him. In October, Mankind introduced Mr. Socko, a sweatsock that he pulled over his hand before clamping on the mandible claw. Mankind's relationship with McMahon became closer. Mankind started calling his boss "Dad."

But "Dad" couldn't be trusted. The world title was declared vacant and put up for grabs in a tournament at the 1998 Survivor Series on November 15 in St. Louis. Mankind beat Duane Gill in the first round and Al Snow in the second round. In the semifinals, Mankind went up against Austin. Stone Cold was outbrawling Mankind and had him covered for a pin, but Shane McMahon, serving as referee, stopped counting at two. As Austin stared at Shane in disbelief, Gerald Brisco flattened Austin with a chair, allowing Mankind to score the pin and advance in the tournament.

The championship match was a showdown between Mankind and Rocky Maivia. Mankind and the fans were shocked when the Rock locked Mankind in a sharpshooter leglock, and McMahon immediately called for the bell. Mankind had never submitted. After the match, Maivia hugged McMahon. Mankind had been double-crossed.

Mankind was dead-set on revenge. At General Motors Place in Vancouver, British

Mankind liked to put a white athletic sock he called "Mr. Socko" on his hand before giving his opponents the mandible claw.

Columbia, on December 13, Mankind busted a few of the Rock's ribs before the card, then gave every member of McMahon's entourage, including Vince, the mandible claw.

But the ultimate revenge was gained on December 29, 1998, when Mankind and the Rock squared off in Worcester, Massachusetts. That night, Mankind beat the Rock for his first WWF World title.

Mick Foley, a.k.a. Mankind, was world champion.

THE FOUR FACES
OF FOLEY

6

Years ago, being WWF World champion was a long-term proposition. Bruno Sammartino's first world title reign, beginning in 1963, lasted nearly eight years. Hulk Hogan's first world title reign, beginning in 1984, lasted more than four years. But in today's tumultuous world of professional wrestling, world title reigns last months, weeks, and sometimes even days.

The war between Mankind and the Rock intensified. They met again in an "I Quit" match at the 1999 Royal Rumble. This time, the Rock was out for revenge. He assaulted Mankind with violent kicks and punches. The champion absorbed a horrendous beating. The Rock smashed Mankind through an announcers' table and later sent him careening off a balcony and through an electric console 12 feet below. The two men used the ringside microphone, timekeeper's bell, and a ladder on each other. Mankind dug in, willing to take as much punishment as necessary. He refused to submit. Then, as the Rock slammed him over the head 10 times with a steel chair, the words "I quit" were heard over the arena sound system.

"Come on, fellas," Mankind said afterward. "That was obviously a piped-in voice. Somehow they got me on tape saying those words. Mankind doesn't quit."

Mankind faces down the Rock, who finally defeated him at the 1999 Royal Rumble after the McMahons played a tape of Mankind saying "I quit."

Although it was later learned that the McMahons and their cronies had taped Mankind saying "I quit" at another time, Mankind couldn't do anything to reverse the decision. Vince McMahon was the man in charge, and he wasn't concerned about the integrity of the world title. All he was concerned about was making sure that his man was the champion.

"After the first few shots, I'm not sure I felt that much or even remember that much," Mankind told *Pro Wrestling Illustrated* magazine. "All I knew was that I was not going to give in, no matter how much pain I was going through."

It was probably of no consolation to Mankind that the match was named Match of the Year by the readers of *Pro Wrestling Illustrated*. Mankind and the Rock met again on January 26, 1999, in an empty arena in Tucson, Arizona. Their match was aired live on cable's USA Network during halftime of the Super Bowl. Mankind and the Rock battled all over the arena, including in a cafeteria and in and out of several offices. Finally, they brawled onto the loading dock of the Tucson Convention Center, and Mankind used a forklift to lower beer kegs onto the Rock. Maivia was helpless. Mankind scored the pin to become a two-time world champion.

Mankind and the Rock intensified their battle. After a match on February 14, 1999, at the St. Valentine's Day Massacre pay-per-view, both men had to be taken away in an ambulance. The match was ruled a draw.

Mankind vs. the Rock had become one of the most emotional feuds in wrestling history,

and both men were easily goaded into doing things they didn't want to do. At *Monday Night Raw* on February 15, the Rock demanded a rematch. Mankind refused. Finally, the Rock insulted him into accepting a ladder match that night.

When the bell rang, the Rock choked Mankind with a television cable. Mankind responded by throwing the metal ring steps at him. Maivia reversed a piledriver, flattening the announcer's table. As both men climbed the ladder, a new wrestler came onto the scene: Paul Wight, who had wrestled in WCW as the Giant. He was there to help the Rock. Wight chokeslammed Mankind off of the ladder and the Rock retrieved the belt. After the match, both the Rock and Wight attacked Mankind.

Because Steve Austin had won the right to battle the world champion in the main event of

Mankind defeated Triple H and Stone Cold for his third WWF World title at a SummerSlam '99 triple threat match refereed by former WWF wrestler and governor of Minnesota Jesse Ventura.

WrestleMania XV, Mankind was left in an unusual position: He and Wight would battle in a match early in the card to decide who would referee Austin vs. Maivia. Of course, McMahon wanted Wight to be the referee, and he was enraged when Wight, who had beaten Mankind, was then disqualified for powerbombing him after the bell.

Mankind was in bad shape from the power-bomb and had to be taken to a nearby hospital. It seemed doubtful he'd be able to referee Austin vs. the Rock. McMahon appointed him-self the referee for the match, but WWF commissioner Shawn Michaels said, "Not so fast." Earl Hebner was named referee for the bout. Late in the match between Austin and the Rock, Mankind hobbled to the ring and made the three-count on Austin's victory over the Rock. McMahon had been foiled again.

Now Mankind was feuding with Paul Wight and the entire McMahon family. He beat Wight in a boiler room brawl on April 25, 1999, but afterward was attacked by Big Bossman and Test. He formed an anti-Shane McMahon group called the Union, but suffered another serious injury when Hunter Hearst Helmsley hit him over the knee with a sledgehammer. As a result of the injury, Mankind was sidelined for six weeks.

The injuries were piling up. Although he had wrestled as Mankind, Cactus Jack, and Dude Love, Mick Foley only had one body, and it had sustained too much punishment over too short a period of time.

"My knees are still a little sore, so don't expect too much crazy stuff from me," Mankind said upon his return to the ring in late July.

"Just a lot of good, solid mat wrestling. I won't be climbing any cages for a while."

But there was still a lot of courage left in Mankind's battered body. At SummerSlam '99 on August 22, Mankind squared off with Triple-H and Austin in a triple-threat match for Austin's world title. Jesse Ventura, the governor of Minnesota, was the guest referee. Mankind was at a severe disadvantage. He was attacked by Chyna, Triple-H's bodyguard. Triple-H laid out both Austin and Mankind with a chair, but Ventura refused to count Triple-H's pin of Mankind. Triple-H nearly pinned Austin, but Mankind stopped the pin attempt and nailed Austin with a double-arm DDT. Mankind covered Austin for the pin. He had become three-time WWF World champion.

"This is a dream come true," Mankind said. "Now I'm a three-time WWF champion. Everyone counted me out of this match because I was coming off a real serious injury, but I showed 'em all what I was made of. Helmsley calls himself 'the Game,' but he doesn't have any. Austin says, 'Don't trust anybody,' so I didn't. That's why I'm the champion today."

The title reign lasted one day. The next night at *Raw* in Ames, Iowa, Triple-H beat Mankind for the world title.

Despite the loss, Mankind's popularity was at an all-time high. He put aside his differences with the Rock and formed the Rock 'n' Sock Connection. Mankind and the Rock beat the Undertaker and the Big Show (Paul Wight) for the world tag team title on August 30, 1999. They lost the belts seven days later, and regained them again for a day. Mankind and the Rock became three-time world tag team champions with a victory over the New Age Outlaws on October 12, 1999, and nearly a month later Mankind teamed with Al Snow to win another world tag team title. Their reign lasted six days.

Mankind had become a national phenomenon. He appeared in humorous television ads for Chef Boyardee. His autobiography, *Have a Nice Day*, soared to the top of the *New York Times* bestseller list, an incredible achievement for a professional wrestler.

Ironically, Mankind reached the top of his profession at the same time he decided to slow down. He was tired of putting his body on the line every night. His wife and children feared for his life. He had suffered several concussions and knew that if he didn't start taking care of his body, he'd never grow old enough to see his children get married or play with his grandchildren.

Late in 1999 Triple-H and his new wife, Stephanie McMahon, gained control of the WWF and ordered the Rock and Mankind to wrestle in a pink-slip-on-a-pole match. The loser would get fired from the federation. On December 27, 1999, Mankind lost the match. His career appeared to be over.

But with Mankind gone, Cactus Jack returned.

And a new Mankind showed up: a fake Mankind, who made unflattering remarks about Mick Foley's wife. Foley charged out, beat up the fake Mankind, and left him lying in the ring.

On January 23, 2000, at the Royal Rumble, Cactus Jack lost to Triple-H in a street fight, but the match didn't end when the final bell rang. As Triple-H was being carried from the ring on a stretcher, Cactus Jack attacked him with a two-by-four wrapped in barbed-wire.

Little by little, the in-the-ring activity of the various faces of Mick Foley lessened. At the end of January, Cactus Jack invited some old friends from WCW—Chris Benoit, Dean Malenko, Eddy Guerrero, and Perry Saturn—to the WWF. In February, Cactus Jack publicly stated that he was considering retirement because of the injuries he had suffered. He announced that his Hell In A Cell match against Triple-H at No Way Out on February 27, 2000, would be his last.

"Come No Way Out, Triple-H is going to find himself surrounded by photographers scram-

As WWF commissioner, Mick Foley made sure his old enemies had a difficult time succeeding in the federation.

bling to get shots of his broken, beaten, bloody body," Cactus said. "If he thought he shed a lot of blood at the Royal Rumble, he has no idea what's in store for him now. Cactus Jack is waiting for him."

At No Way Out, Cactus assaulted Triple-H from the opening bell. During the match, Cactus fell off of the cage. Then he lit the barbed wire on fire and drove it into Triple-H's face. When the cage broke, Cactus fell through and the ring broke in half. Triple-H went on to win the match and retain the world title. Cactus Jack refused medical help, but was crying as he left the ring to a standing ovation from the crowd.

Had the wrestling world seen the last of Mick Foley?

Not by a longshot.

When Triple-H, the Rock, and the Big Show signed for a three-way match at WrestleMania XVI—with Stephanie McMahon, Vince McMahon, and Shane McMahon in their respective corners, Linda McMahon—Vince's wife— announced that the three-way match would be a "Fatal Four Way" elimination match. The fourth wrestler would be Mick Foley, and Linda McMahon would be in his corner.

But WrestleMania XVI would not be a victorious last hurrah for Foley. He was the second man eliminated by Triple-H.

Again, however, the wrestling world had not seen the last of Mick Foley.

On June 26, 2000, Mick Foley was introduced as the new commissioner of the WWF. He was a controversial, hands-on commissioner, ordering his former enemies, such as Triple-H, to participate in difficult matches, and almost single-handedly stopping Steve Austin from running roughshod over the federation.

As 2000 drew to a close, the wrestling world wondered if it would ever see Mick Foley—or Cactus Jack, or Mankind, or Dude Love—step into a wrestling ring as an active competitor again. The answer, considering his bruised and battered body, should probably be no. Yet, as his career has shown, anything is possible. Just when this incredible competitor is counted down and out, he rises yet again to prove himself resilient and victorious.

There can be no doubt that wrestling is in Mick Foley's blood, just as, for the past decade and a half, Mick Foley's blood has been all over wrestling.

Chronology

1965   Born Mick Foley in Setauket, New York on June 7

1986   Makes his professional wrestling debut as Cactus Jack

1987   Graduates from the University of New York at Cortland College and goes on his first pro wrestling tour of Africa

1988   The Wrestling Observer newsletter calls him "the best no-name independent in the country"; Cactus Jack and Gary Young capture the CWA tag team title in Evansville, Indiana in October

1989   Makes his debut in WCW

1990   Gets up after being dropkicked onto the concrete floor by Mil Mascaras on February 6; battles Eddie Gilbert in a violent best-of-three-falls match at Tri-State's Summer Sizzler Card on August 3; returns to WCW at Clash of the Champions XVI on September 5 and attacks Sting

1993   Gets powerbombed onto a concrete floor by Big Van Vader and suffers a concussion and temporary amnesia on April 21

1994   Wins the WCW tag team title with Kevin Sullivan on May 22; loses a loser-leaves-WCW bout to Kevin Sullivan on September 18; Wins the ECW tag team title with Mikey Whipwreck on August 27

1996   Debuts in the WWF as Mankind in March; introduces the Mandible Claw

1997   Mick Foley introduces Dude Love to the WWF in May

1998   Loses to the Undertaker on June 28; Vince McMahon double-crosses Mankind, who loses to Rocky Maivia in the finals of the WWF World title tournament on November 15; beats the Rock for his first WWF World heavyweight title on December 29

1999   Beats the Rock for his second WWF World title on January 26; defeats Triple-H and Steve Austin for his third WWF World title on August 22; loses a pink-slip-on-a-pole match to the Rock and is forced to retire on December 27

2000   Wrestles his last match as Cactus Jack and loses to Triple-H on February 27; named commissioner of the WWF on January 26

Further Reading

Burkett, Harry. "Wrestle-McMania! Power . . . Greed . . . Pride." *Pro Wrestling Illustrated* (September 2000): 19–21.

Ethier, Bryan. "When Will Mankind Finally Tell the Rock ... `Put a Sock In It!'" *The Wrestler* (February 2000): 34–37.

Foley, Mick. *Mankind: Have a Nice Day! A Tale of Blood and Sweatsocks.* New York: Regan Books/Harper Collins, 1999.

"Match of the Year: The Undertaker vs. Mankind." *Pro Wrestling Illustrated* (March 1999): 53.

Rosenbaum, David. "Every Day's a Nice Day for Mick Foley." *The Wrestler* (January 2001): 32–35.

"Supercards 2000: Exclusive Coverage of 2000's Greatest Events." *Pro Wrestling Illustrated* (August 2000): 18–23.

Index

Photo Credits
Associated Press/WWP: p. 53; Jeff Eisenberg Sports Photography: pp. 10, 15, 18, 20, 25, 31, 35, 38, 45, 50; Howard Kernats Photography: pp. 2, 28, 49, 57, 60; Sports Action: pp. 6, 8, 42.

KYLE ALEXANDER has been involved in the publication of professional wrestling magazines for more than a decade. His previously published volumes about professional wrestling include *The Story of the Wrestler They Call " Sting"* and *Bill Goldberg*. Over the past 10 years, he has made numerous appearances on radio and television, offering his unique perspective on the "sport of kings."